The Three Musketeers

Alexandre Dumas

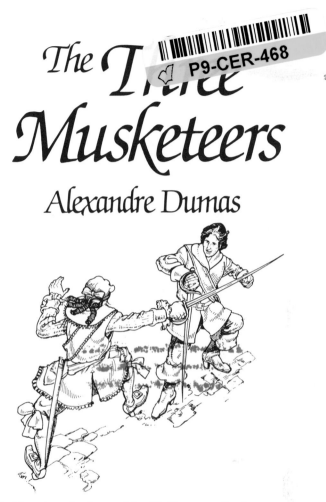

Abridged and adapted by T. Ernesto Bethancourt

Illustrated by James McConnell

A PACEMAKER CLASSIC

FEARON/JANUS
Belmont, California

Simon & Schuster Supplementary Education Group

Other Pacemaker Classics

The Adventures of Huckleberry Finn
The Adventures of Tom Sawyer
A Christmas Carol
Crime and Punishment
The Deerslayer
Dr. Jekyll and Mr. Hyde
Ethan Frome
Frankenstein
Great Expectations
Jane Eyre
The Jungle Book
The Last of the Mohicans
Moby Dick
The Moonstone
The Red Badge of Courage
Robinson Crusoe
The Scarlet Letter
A Tale of Two Cities
The Time Machine
Treasure Island
20,000 Leagues Under the Sea
Two Years Before the Mast
Wuthering Heights

Library of Congress Catalog Card Number: 86-81453

ISBN 0–8224–9261–X

Printed in the United States of America

10 9 8 7 6 5

Contents

Introduction v

1 The Man in Meung 1

2 D'Artagnan Meets M. de Tréville 6

3 Dueling with Musketeers 17

4 A Job at Hand 24

5 To the Rescue 29

6 The Cardinal's Plot 38

7 Journey to London 46

8 The King's Ball 52

9 Milady 57

10 Justice Done 64

Introduction

The Three Musketeers is an exciting, romantic tale set in France during the 1600s. Its main character, D'Artagnan, was an actual person. The author, Alexandre Dumas, based much of *The Three Musketeers* on D'Artagnan's real-life adventures.

The story concerns D'Artagnan's desire to become one of the guardsmen of the King of France. Soon after arriving in Paris, D'Artagnan meets Athos, Porthos, and Aramis. These three Musketeers are three of the best-known fighters of the day. The three men welcome D'Artagnan into their group, and their amazing adventures form the story that Dumas tells.

Alexandre Dumas was born in France in 1802. His father was a general in Napoleon's army. Dumas became a well-known playwright before he began to write novels. In addition to *The Three Musketeers*, Dumas also wrote another famous historical novel, *The Count of Monte Cristo*. Both books are filled with exciting action and colorful characters. They have remained very popular with readers of all ages for more than 140 years.

1 The Man in Meung

On the first Monday in April of the year 1625, an eighteen-year-old man left home and rode toward Paris, France, to find his fortune. His name was D'Artagnan. His clothes were old and worn. And so was his horse. It was an old farm horse, yellow in color. It didn't have a single hair on its tail. But if you were to laugh at this country boy or his horse, it would have been a bad mistake.

D'Artagnan, for all his country looks, was no farmer. His father had been a brave soldier who served the King of France for many years. He had taught his son all he knew about sword fighting. He had even given D'Artagnan his old sword. And the young man knew how to use it well.

D'Artagnan had a quick temper. He was from a part of France called Gascony. The people from Gascony are known for two things: being brave and not taking anything from anybody . . . at any time.

D'Artagnan was a Gascon from his cap, with a long feather in it, to the bottoms of his well-worn boots. He was brown from the sun, and he had a big Gascon nose. But he was as quick to laugh as he was to fight. He didn't have much besides his

1

sword, his horse, and his pride. His father had given him fifteen gold coins and a letter.

The letter was to M. de Tréville, the man in charge of the King's Musketeers. The King's Musketeers were the best fighters in France, and D'Artagnan's father had served them well. Young D'Artagnan wanted to join the Musketeers, and the letter would help him.

D'Artagnan was tired. He had been on the road a long time. Paris was still many miles away. So, when he came to the town of Meung, he thought he'd stay at the inn there. As he rode up to the inn, he saw three men through the ground-floor window. One of them seemed to be the head man. He was well dressed, and he had a scar on his left brow. The men were talking and laughing.

Now, D'Artagnan knew how silly he looked, with his funny horse and farmer's clothes. When he heard the men laughing, he thought they were making fun of him. His Gascon temper ran hot. He walked up to the window, with his hand on his sword.

"You . . . behind the shutter," he said. "What's so funny? If it's a joke, we can all laugh together."

The well-dressed man looked at D'Artagnan as if he were dirt. He came out from the inn, and D'Artagnan got a better look at him. He was in his late thirties, the boy guessed. And he looked mean, with the scar on his face.

"That's some horse," the man said in a nasty tone. "I've seen many yellow flowers, but never a yellow horse. Was its father a buttercup?"

He was going to say more, but he didn't get the chance. D'Artagnan had his sword out in a flash. The man jumped back, or he would have been stuck like a frog. He drew his own sword. D'Artagnan stood ready to fight.

But the man's two friends had come out of the inn, unseen by D'Artagnan. They came up behind him with sticks and a shovel. One of them caught D'Artagnan on the side of the head. He reeled, but it didn't drop him. D'Artagnan fought like a tiger. But in the end, three against one was too much for him.

When he woke up, he was in a bed inside the inn. There was a bandage on his head, and he hurt all over. Even though it was hard, he got out of bed. The first thing he did was check his money bag. The fifteen gold coins were still there. But his letter to M. de Tréville was gone!

"My letter!" he cried. "I must find my letter!"

He made his way down the stairs to the kitchen. The man who ran the inn was there with his wife.

"Ah, thank God you are better!" the man cried.

"Where is my letter?" demanded D'Artagnan. He reached to his side. It was then he noticed his sword was gone. "And where is my sword?"

"It was broken by the men you fought," the man replied. "And they took your letter, too."

"But who were they?" cried D'Artagnan. "They will pay for this. In blood!"

"They did not give their names," the man answered. "I am a poor keeper of an inn. They paid me well, and I didn't ask any questions. But they went toward Paris."

"Then, so will I," said D'Artagnan. "And when I find them . . ."

2 D'Artagnan Meets M. de Tréville

When D'Artagnan reached Paris, the first thing he did was sell his ugly horse. Until he got a job with the King's Musketeers, he would need all the money he could get. He already had spent some of his gold on a new sword. For a fighting man in those days would never be without a blade.

The next thing he did was look for a place to live. He found a cheap two-room apartment. All it had was a bed, a table, and a chair. But the price was right. He gave the landlord, M. Bonacieux, enough rent for a month. Then he went off to the royal palace to find M. de Tréville, the head of the King's Musketeers.

As he walked the streets of Paris, D'Artagnan realized why the man with the scar had laughed. The young man had never seen so many finely dressed people. They were everywhere, rushing back and forth, and in and out of buildings. And the buildings were taller than any D'Artagnan had ever seen.

When he finally found the palace, he asked for M. de Tréville. The guard at the gate laughed. "You must be a country boy," the guard said. "M. de

Tréville doesn't *live* here. His Musketeers work here. He has a hotel all to himself."

"Then he must be an important man," D'Artagnan said. He felt like fighting with the guard over the country boy remark. But he was lost in a strange city. He stayed calm.

"Important?" the guard said. "Why, young man, there are only two other men in France as important as M. de Tréville. The Cardinal Richelieu, and the King himself!" The guard looked around, as if he were afraid someone would hear. "And sometimes, they say, the Cardinal and M. de Tréville are more important than the King."

The guard gave D'Artagnan good directions. After a short walk, the young Gascon was at M. de Tréville's hotel. You could tell right away that this was the home of the head Musketeer. All around the block were brave men at arms. They were drinking at cafés, laughing, and carrying on. All wore the uniform of the King's Musketeers.

D'Artagnan later found out why there were so many armed men around the hotel. M. de Tréville was such a big man in France that he had many enemies. The man who was after his power most was Cardinal Richelieu. And Richelieu had his own guards—all brave fighting men, too. But they were not as brave or good as the Musketeers. Very often—even though they weren't supposed to—the

Musketeers fought with Richelieu's men. And almost always, they won.

In the middle of the crowd of armed men, one man caught D'Artagnan's eye. He was a giant for those days, well over six feet tall. And he was dressed differently from the others. Over his regular uniform, he wore a long red cape. His sword belt, hanging from his shoulder, was bright blue and gold. Even the sword he carried was oversized.

This giant man was laughing and talking with another Musketeer who was very handsome. He was like a prince in a storybook. They seemed to be having a great time. D'Artagnan stood close and listened to them. He learned that the giant's name was Porthos, and that the good-looking young man was named Aramis. He also noticed that Aramis knew how handsome he was. He was always posing, showing himself off.

D'Artagnan finally found a servant, who gave him directions on how to find M. de Tréville. The man led him to a huge room, where many others waited. "The guard was right," D'Artagnan thought. "M. de Tréville *is* important. Look at all these fine people waiting to see him. I'm going to have a long, long wait."

But he gave his name to the servant, sat down on the bench, and hoped for the best. You can imagine his surprise when the servant came out of De Tréville's office a few minutes later and called out, "M. d'Artagnan . . . the Captain of the King's Musketeers will see you!"

D'Artagnan got to his feet and crossed the big room. All the richly dressed men stared at him. He laughed a bit to himself. "I may look like a farmer," he thought, "but my father's name still carries weight in Paris. After all, he was once the best swordsman in France!"

M. de Tréville's office was as big as the outside room. Everything in it looked as if it had cost a fortune. The Captain of the King's Musketeers was a short, heavyset man. He was about fifty years old—the same age as D'Artagnan's father. And he greeted the young Gascon as he would his own son.

"Sit down, my boy, sit down," De Tréville said. "When the servant said M. d'Artagnan, I thought it was your father, coming to visit. What brings you to Paris?"

D'Artagnan told his story to M. de Tréville. When D'Artagnan got to the part about the man with the scar, De Tréville frowned. "You have made a very powerful enemy, young man," he said. "I know this fellow with the scar."

"He is a thief and a coward!" cried D'Artagnan, getting to his feet, his hand on his sword.

"Quiet down," the older man said. "He is no coward. He is a brave man and one of the best

swordsmen in France. He works for Cardinal Richelieu. He could have killed you while you were knocked out. But he didn't. He probably thought you a country boy, not worth getting his sword bloody on. You were quite lucky."

"His luck will run out when I catch him," D'Artagnan said. "He will taste cold steel. Tell me his name, sir."

"I will do no such thing," De Tréville said. "I have enough trouble right now with the Cardinal's men." He paused and looked at some papers on his desk. "That reminds me," he said. "I have to take care of some business right away. It will only take a few minutes. You can stay here and listen. Perhaps when you hear this, you will understand what I have to deal with."

He rang a bell on his desk. The servant came in. "Tell Athos, Porthos, and Aramis to come in," said De Tréville. To D'Artagnan, he said, "Stay in the dark corner over there, out of sight."

Into De Tréville's office came the three Musketeers: Porthos, the giant D'Artagnan had seen, Aramis, the handsome one, and another, a stranger to D'Artagnan. He, too, was handsome. He was dark haired and had a short beard. He walked like a man of importance—as if he were a duke or a count. D'Artagnan knew that many men of noble birth served in the Musketeers.

This man was very pale, and his walk was not steady. At first, D'Artagnan thought he might be drunk. Then he saw that the man was wounded. But for all his pain, he stood up straight, alongside the others.

M. de Tréville's face showed anger. He began to pace up and down in front of the men, who stayed at attention. "What am I going to do with you three?" he said, angrily. "Fighting again! Two of the Cardinal's men are dead!"

"There would have been more," said Porthos, the giant, "but they didn't fight fairly. They came

up behind us. Before Athos could get his sword out, he was wounded. We did our best—"

"And you were arrested for fighting," snapped De Tréville. "You know it is against the law for French soldiers to fight each other. Now if you had gotten away . . ."

Just at that second, Athos fell to the floor. His friends flew to his side. "They left him for dead, sir," Aramis said.

In a second De Tréville's anger was gone. He dropped to his knees, at Athos's side. He looked at the wound. Even from where he stood, D'Artagnan could see it was serious. De Tréville spoke softly to the fallen Athos, but D'Artagnan could not hear what he said. Then De Tréville got to his feet.

"Very well," the Captain of the Musketeers said. "There will be no punishment for you men. But this fighting with the Cardinal's men must stop. France needs her brave men too much to waste them on each other. You may go. And see that Athos gets the best of care." The older man smiled. "And send the doctor bills to me."

Once the Musketeers had gone, De Tréville turned to D'Artagnan. "You see what I must deal with, my boy? The Cardinal's men sneak up on my Musketeers. They try to kill them. Then, when they lose some of their own, they come crying like babies. They want me to punish my own men, for being brave!"

"I don't understand, sir," D'Artagnan said. "Why does this fighting go on? Don't we all serve the King of France?"

"It's supposed to be that way," De Tréville answered. "But what in life is what it's supposed to be? His Majesty, King Louis XIII, would be a good king, if he knew the truth. One man, close to him, tells him lies. He uses the King to get rich and to gain power. This man gives parties for the King. He sends beautiful women his way—spies. Half the time the King doesn't read the papers he signs. The King trusts this man. And I am the only threat to him."

"Cardinal Richelieu?" asked D'Artagnan.

"Never say that aloud!" cried De Tréville. "It could cost you your life. I mentioned no names. And that, dear boy, is why I gave you no name for the man with the scar. He is the number-one man serving Richelieu. I order you to forget about what happened."

He went to his desk, sat down, and began to write. "This is a letter to the King. He does listen to me, now and then. I'll ask that you be admitted to the Royal Academy."

"I'll be a Musketeer?" cried D'Artagnan, in joy.

"Don't be a fool," De Tréville said quickly. "A boy doesn't become a Musketeer his first day in Paris. That is an honor you must earn. To become one of my men, you must first join the King's army as a cadet." Seeing the sad look on D'Artagnan's face, he added, "Then we'll see how you get on. Knowing your father as I do, I'm sure it won't be long. . . . Are you listening to me, young man?"

Indeed, D'Artagnan was not. He was staring out the window at the street below. His face grew pale with anger. His hand flew to his sword.

"What is it?" asked De Tréville. "What do you see in the street?"

"It is the man with the scar," D'Artagnan cried, rushing from the room. "And he won't escape me this time!"

3 Dueling with Musketeers

D'Artagnan ran down the stairs from M. de Tréville's office. He was in such a rush that he ran right into Athos, who was on his way home after having his wound dressed by a doctor. He grabbed D'Artagnan by his long scarf. "You're in a big hurry, young man," he said.

"Let me go!" cried D'Artagnan.

"I can see by your clothes that you are from far away," said Athos, not letting D'Artagnan go. "But did you leave all of your good manners behind?"

"If I weren't in such a hurry," D'Artagnan said, "I'd show you some manners." His hand went to his sword.

"I'm not hard to find," said Athos. He was saying that he'd fight D'Artagnan anytime.

"Where?" asked D'Artagnan.

"The convent of Carmes-Deschaux," said Athos.

"What time?"

"About noon," Athos replied.

"Good," said D'Artagnan. "I'll be there. Now will you let me go?"

"With pleasure," said Athos.

D'Artagnan ran down the stairs and toward the hotel gate. Porthos was there, talking with another Musketeer. D'Artagnan tried to run right between them. But just then, a wind came up. It blew Porthos's fancy cape in the air, and D'Artagnan ran right into it.

"What is this?" cried Porthos. "A crazy man?"

"I'm not crazy," said D'Artagnan. "But I am in a hurry." He looked at Porthos. The giant's cape was thrown over his shoulders. D'Artagnan saw that while Porthos wore a rich cape, he had a patch on the seat of his pants. D'Artagnan smiled. "You surprise me, sir," he said. "For one so rich in front, you seem poor behind!"

"You'll pay for that!" cried Porthos, grabbing at his sword. But D'Artagnan was already away and running.

"Fine," cried D'Artagnan, over his shoulder. "Any place you say."

"At one o'clock, behind the Luxembourg palace!" shouted Porthos after D'Artagnan.

"I'll be there," called D'Artagnan. He ran into the street. But the man with the scar was gone. Angry that he'd lost him, D'Artagnan headed back to his new rooms.

On his way, he came across Aramis. The handsome Musketeer was talking with some of the King's guards. D'Artagnan saw that Aramis had dropped a fancy handkerchief. He didn't seem to

know it. D'Artagnan bent over and picked it up. He handed it to Aramis.

"Here, you dropped this," D'Artagnan said.

"I dropped nothing," replied Aramis.

"Are you calling me a liar?" said D'Artagnan, getting angry.

"I am calling you a fool," said the handsome Musketeer. "Can't you see it's a woman's handkerchief? And now you have brought her name into my talk with these men. Clearly, you are a farmer with no manners."

"I see," said D'Artagnan. "And you think you can teach me some?"

"Someone has to," said Aramis. "Meet me at the hotel of M. de Tréville at two o'clock. Then I will tell you where we shall fight."

D'Artagnan went his way. "Surely I am done for," he thought. "I have to fight three men today. And all of them are Musketeers. But if I am killed, at least it will be by a Musketeer!"

He looked up at a nearby church clock. It was almost noon. He took the road to Carmes-Deschaux, where he would fight Athos. It was a long walk to the convent. When he got there, he found Athos waiting. He was sitting on a rock. D'Artagnan waved to him.

"About time," said Athos. "But no matter. My two seconds aren't here yet."

D'Artagnan knew what Athos was talking about. In those days, when gentlemen dueled with swords, they always brought friends. When a man was hurt, his friends took care of him—or his dead body. They also made sure that the fight was fair. These men were called *seconds*.

Just as Athos was speaking, his seconds showed up. They were Porthos and Aramis! "Wait!" cried Porthos. "*I* am fighting this man!"

"Not until one o'clock," said D'Artagnan, with a smile.

"But *I* am fighting him!" cried Aramis.

"Not until I fight those two," said D'Artagnan.

"You're pretty sure of yourself," said Porthos, laughing.

"My father was the best swordsman in France," said D'Artagnan, with pride.

"Then he'll be sorry to hear you're dead," said Athos, taking out his sword.

"I hate to kill a man who's already hurt," said D'Artagnan. "Do you want to change your mind?"

"What?" cried Athos. "I could fight you if I were already dead! *En garde!*"

Before they could go at it, a voice shouted: "Stop in the name of Cardinal Richelieu!" All four men turned. Five of the Cardinal's men, with swords drawn, were coming at them. "It is against the law to duel!" shouted the captain of Richelieu's men.

Athos turned to D'Artagnan with a smile. "You must excuse us, young man," he said. "It seems that before I can kill you, I must take care of those fools over there."

Porthos and Aramis drew their swords, too. "A good warm-up for my duel with you," said Athos to D'Artagnan. "Even if it is five against three here."

"Five against *four*," cried D'Artagnan, as he took his place next to the three Musketeers. "I am with you!"

They fought like tigers. In no time, D'Artagnan had run his sword through the captain of Richelieu's men. He quickly got another. The three Musketeers watched, their eyes wide. Then they all fought the three men who were left. Before long, they had won the fight.

Porthos roared with laughter. "Maybe it's just as well we did not fight each other, young man," he said to D'Artagnan. "I would hate to have killed one so brave."

"And I," said Athos and Aramis, together. "Besides," added Athos, "I'm not so sure one of *us* wouldn't have been hurt."

They all laughed. Athos threw his arm over D'Artagnan's shoulder. Arm in arm, they walked off to tell M. de Tréville of their victory.

4 A Job at Hand

From that day on, Athos, Porthos, and Aramis treated D'Artagnan as if he were one of them. But it was Porthos, who always cared about the way people dressed, who took D'Artagnan in hand.

"Your trouble is that you look like a farmer," he told D'Artagnan. "We must teach you to look, act, and dress like a Musketeer."

"How do I do that?" asked D'Artagnan. "I have very little money."

"Who doesn't?" said Aramis. "We're all poor. To be a Musketeer is a great honor. But it doesn't pay well."

"No matter," Porthos said. "There are ways to get around that. First, you need a lackey—someone to wait on you. All of us have lackeys. You must have one, too. As for your clothes, soon you will get your uniform—a newer one than ours, I might add."

"And what would I pay a lackey with?" asked D'Artagnan.

Porthos laughed. "The streets are full of men with no homes and no food. Any one of them would be glad for a warm, dry place to sleep." As they walked through the streets of Paris, they came to one of the many bridges that cross the river Seine. "Look at that fellow over there," said Porthos.

Standing by the edge of the bridge was a short, ugly man. He was passing the time by spitting into the river and watching the spit make circles in the water. "He looks like a fool," said D'Artagnan.

"The very thing you need," said Porthos, with a smile. "Only a fool would work for a Musketeer with no money!" Porthos was right. They talked to the man. His name was Planchet. To D'Artagnan's surprise, Planchet took the job. He turned out to be a very good man, who would serve D'Artagnan well.

But things weren't going well for the four friends. They were running out of money. Aramis, who always said that one day he would become a priest, even sold some of his books on religion. D'Artagnan was sitting alone in his room, trying to think of a way to make some money, when someone knocked on the door. It was Bonacieux, the man who owned the building. He was a short, fat man, with gray hair. He looked upset.

"I have heard," the man said, "that you are a very brave young man. That you beat two of the Cardinal's best men."

"That is true," D'Artagnan said. "What of it?"

"I need someone like you," Bonacieux said. "My beautiful young wife has been carried off. She sews

for the Queen. Yesterday, on her way home, some men grabbed her. I'd like you to get her back for me. And since you haven't paid your rent in three months . . ."

D'Artagnan's hand went to his sword. "Who are these men?"

"I don't know their names," said the fat man. "But a week ago, my wife pointed one of them out to me. She said he is one of the Cardinal's men."

"Would you know him if you saw him again?" asked D'Artagnan.

"Oh, yes," said Bonacieux. "How could I forget that face? He has a scar—"

"A scar?" asked D'Artagnan, jumping to his feet. "Does he have a nasty way about him?"

"That is the man!" cried Bonacieux.

"But tell me," said D'Artagnan, "why would this man take your wife?"

"She is very close to the Queen," the fat man said. "The Queen may have told her secrets. And everyone knows that the Cardinal will do anything to make trouble for the Queen. That way, the King won't even trust his own wife. Only Richelieu."

"I see," said D'Artagnan. He remembered what M. de Tréville had told him about the Cardinal. "Very well," he said. "I'll do everything I can to save your wife." *And get even with the man with the scar*, he thought.

"Oh, thank you!" cried Bonacieux. "If you can help, you can stay here forever. Rent-free!" The man was still thanking D'Artagnan as he went out the door.

A little while after Bonacieux left, the three Musketeers came to D'Artagnan's room. He quickly told them the story. "We're with you!" cried Porthos. "All for one, and one for all!"

"Yes, but we need a plan," said Athos. "Maybe we should go to our own places and do some serious thinking. We will be in great danger. From now on, we'll be up against Cardinal Richelieu— the second most powerful man in France!"

The others agreed. But as they were getting ready to go, they heard a noise coming from the street. They looked out the window. Some of the Cardinal's soldiers had hold of Bonacieux. They were taking him off.

"I must save Bonacieux," said D'Artagnan.

"No, don't," said Athos. "If you do, the Cardinal will know we're against him in this. The less the Cardinal knows, the better off we are."

"True," said D'Artagnan.

"Then, there you are," said Porthos, with a laugh. "Bonacieux is one less person to worry about. We know where he is. In jail. Now, we'd all better go home."

5 To the Rescue

The next day, Planchet brought some news to D'Artagnan. It seemed that the Cardinal's men were inside the very house where D'Artagnan lived.

"It's a trap, sir," Planchet told his master. "The soldiers of Richelieu grab anyone who comes into Bonacieux's rooms. They are right below our feet, as I speak."

D'Artagnan found a loose board in the floor. He pulled it up quietly and looked down. Sure enough, there were soldiers of the Cardinal inside. He listened to their talk, but he learned nothing. They spoke of what soldiers speak of: money, women, drinking, and fighting. He replaced the floorboard.

But later that night, he heard screams coming from downstairs. He ran to the loose board and took a look. The soldiers had hold of one of the prettiest women D'Artagnan had ever seen. She was very upset.

"Let me go!" she cried to the soldiers. "I am Madame Bonacieux. I work for the Queen. If I tell her of this, you'll all be very sorry, indeed!"

That was all D'Artagnan needed to hear. He was ready to run downstairs and cut the Cardinal's

men to pieces. But he remembered Athos's warning. Athos was the smartest of all the four friends. He would know what to do.

"Planchet," D'Artagnan said to his lackey, "go quickly, and get Athos, Porthos, and Aramis. Tell them to bring their swords. . . . Wait!" As D'Artagnan watched, something was going on downstairs. "They are starting to take her away, Planchet! I must save her. I'll go out the window and in through the front door. You take the stairs. And bring the three Musketeers, as fast as you can!"

D'Artagnan crawled out his window. He hung from the sill for a second, and then he dropped to the street, light as a cat. He put his shoulder to the street door. With drawn sword, he rushed into the room. He caught the Cardinal's men by surprise. He cut one, and they all ran like rabbits.

With the cowards on the run, D'Artagnan turned to the lady he'd saved. She was even prettier up close. She had beautiful blue eyes, dark hair, and clear skin. She seemed to be only a year or two older than D'Artagnan. She smiled and held out her hands to him. D'Artagnan fell in love on the spot.

"You have saved me, sir," she said in a sweet low voice. "How can I ever repay you?"

"No need," said D'Artagnan, kissing her hand. "Just to be in the same room with beauty like yours is payment enough, madame."

"But what did those men want?" she asked. "I took them for robbers at first. And where is my husband?"

"Those men are more dangerous than robbers. They are Cardinal Richelieu's men. As for your husband, they took him away yesterday. He is in the Bastille, the prison of Paris."

"Ah, poor Bonacieux!" the lovely lady cried. "He knows nothing at all." But D'Artagnan noticed that she didn't seem all that upset about her husband being in jail.

D'Artagnan knew that Bonacieux was well-to-do. She could have married the fat old man for his money. And with Bonacieux in jail, maybe he had a chance with this beautiful woman!

"But," asked D'Artagnan, "how did you escape?"

"I waited until I was left alone," answered Madame Bonacieux. "Then, I tied some sheets together and let myself down from the window. I came here, thinking to find my husband."

"To place yourself under his protection?"

"No," she answered. "To warn him that he might be arrested."

"We must leave this house," D'Artagnan told Madame Bonacieux. "The soldiers may return with more men, the cowards. I'll take you to the house of my friend Athos. He and my other friends will see that no harm comes to you."

"Very well, anything you say, handsome sir," said Madame Bonacieux. "But after that, you must go to the palace and leave this note with the Queen's valet." She handed him an envelope. "He will get it to the Queen."

D'Artagnan did as Madame Bonacieux asked. He dropped her off at Athos's house. Athos wasn't home, but D'Artagnan was sure he wouldn't mind. Then he took the note to the Queen's valet. On his way back to Athos's house, he saw two people come out of a side street. One wore the uniform of a Musketeer. The other was a woman, dressed in a heavy cloak with a hood that hid her face. He looked closer. It was Madame Bonacieux!

D'Artagnan's hot Gascon temper rose. He had just saved this woman's life, and here she was running around with some Musketeer—maybe a boyfriend. He knew it was stupid to think this way. He had only just met her. But he was jealous. He ran up to them as they passed a street lamp.

"What do you want?" the man asked, pushing D'Artagnan away.

D'Artagnan drew his sword. The man in the Musketeer uniform did, too.

"In the name of God!" cried Madame Bonacieux, getting between the two angry men. "Please, milord," she said to the man in the Musketeer's uniform.

"Milord?" said D'Artagnan. Was this man some high nobleman? "I beg your pardon, sir . . . ," he began.

"This is the Duke of Buckingham," explained Madame Bonacieux. "He is the prime minister of England. He loves the Queen very much. And I am taking him to see her. That is what the note was about. But if Cardinal Richelieu knew he was in France . . ."

"The Queen could be tried for being a traitor," said Buckingham.

"And you may have undone us all, with your temper, M. d'Artagnan," said Madame Bonacieux.

"A thousand pardons," said D'Artagnan. "I had no way of knowing. What can I do to help?"

"Follow us, twenty steps behind," said the Englishman. "Guard our backs. The Cardinal's men are everywhere."

D'Artagnan went with them all the way to the Louvre, the royal palace. Once he saw they were safely inside, he headed back for home.

Madame Bonacieux led Buckingham through a servants' entrance and through some secret passages. Finally, she left him in a secret room. A hidden door opened, and into the room walked Anne of Austria, the Queen of France. Buckingham kneeled and kissed her hand.

"Madame," he said to her, "I love you more than life itself!"

"Why are you doing this?" she asked. "Why do you take these chances? I have never led you on. Even though I love you, I am Queen of France. I cannot cheat on the King."

It was true. Just as Madame Bonacieux was married to a man she didn't love, so was the Queen of France. Her marriage to Louis XIII had been set up without her consent. She did love Buckingham, and he loved her. But they could only steal time together. What made it worse was the danger of war between England and France. If Buckingham were caught in France, he could be killed as a spy.

"You have put your life in danger by coming here," the Queen said.

"I don't care," said Buckingham. "Just to see you for a minute or two is enough. But would you do me one favor?"

"Anything," said Anne.

"Give me something of yours to take with me," said Buckingham. "Anything at all, so that when we're apart, it can remind me of you."

"And will you go, then? Will you get out of this terrible danger?"

The Duke of Buckingham agreed, and the Queen left the room. In a second, she returned with a fancy velvet box. She handed it to the Duke. "Take this," she said. "There's a necklace inside. It's my very favorite. Now, please go, before you're seen!"

The Duke did as the Queen asked. Madame Bonacieux was waiting outside the room. She led him to safety. The Queen, the Duke, and Madame Bonacieux, all without knowing it, had started young D'Artagnan on the greatest adventure of his life.

6 The Cardinal's Plot

Fat little M. Bonacieux sat in a chair in front of the desk of Cardinal Richelieu. It was well that he sat. If he were standing, his knees would have shaken too much. He had been listening to the Cardinal for a long time. Richelieu asked many questions, but poor Bonacieux had few answers.

After a while, Richelieu realized that the little man knew nothing. The Cardinal was a little angry. He had hoped to learn the secrets between Madame Bonacieux and the Queen. It was Richelieu's plan to catch the Queen doing something wrong. That way, the King would trust only Richelieu, making him the most powerful man in France—even more powerful than M. de Tréville.

"I can see you are in the dark," Richelieu said to Bonacieux. "Even about what goes on in your own house. So . . . I'll set you free."

Bonacieux nearly cried, he was so happy. He got up, but the Cardinal froze him with a move of his hand. "One more thing . . . ," said Richelieu.

"Anything . . . anything, sire!" cried Bonacieux.

"You will watch everyone who sees your wife. You will listen to everything she says. You will

write down where she goes, and when. Then you will come and tell me."

"Of course, sire," said Bonacieux. "Whatever you want."

"Good . . . good," said Richelieu, with an oily smile. "Here is some money for you. Those who work for me get paid well. Don't they, Rochefort?" He smiled at a soldier who stood near the door.

That soldier had been making Bonacieux nervous for two weeks. And now he knew his name. Rochefort was the name of the man with the scar. As Bonacieux bowed and backed out of the Cardinal's office, he gave a lot of room to Rochefort.

Once Bonacieux was gone, Richelieu said to Rochefort, "What have you learned?"

"A great deal, sir," said the man with the scar. "I have a spy in the palace. She has been watching Madame Bonacieux and the Queen. Madame Bonacieux brought the Duke of Buckingham to the Queen."

Richelieu's eyes lit up. "I heard he was in France!" he said. "Tell me more, Rochefort."

Rochefort told the Cardinal the whole story. "And inside the box she gave Buckingham," said the man with the scar, "is a diamond necklace. Do you remember it? It's her favorite, sir."

"Of course I recall it," said Richelieu. "It was given to her by the King. It has twelve perfect diamonds." His face grew dark. "And I'm sure it is now in England, in Buckingham's palace."

"It is, sir. The Duke has made it into twelve diamond buttons. He wears them at special parties at his palace. I heard this from our spy in London."

"Ah, yes, the Lady de Winter," said Richelieu. "She has done good work for us. She is the perfect spy. She is so beautiful that men will do anything for her. They will tell her anything." He laughed. "They don't know that Lady de Winter is as cold as ice, and crueler than any man I know."

"Maybe she can steal the diamonds," Rochefort said.

The Cardinal snapped his fingers. "No! I have a much better idea," he said. "Get me a pen and paper, Rochefort."

The Cardinal sat down and wrote a short letter:

Milady,

Be at the next big party the Duke of Buckingham gives. He will be wearing twelve diamond buttons on his jacket. Get close to him, and steal two of them. Once you have them, send word to me.

He gave the letter to Rochefort, who read it.

"I'll see that it gets to Milady right away, sir," Rochefort said.

"Excellent, Rochefort," said the Cardinal. "Now I must go see the King. I have a surprise for him. I have the Queen in my power now!"

"I can't believe what you say, Richelieu," said the King. "The prime minister of England was here, in Paris? Why didn't you arrest him?"

"I couldn't, your majesty," said Richelieu. "I have no proof. The Englishman has powerful friends at the palace."

"You mean the Queen!" cried Louis XIII, his face a mask of anger. "She loves Buckingham. I know she does!"

"We have no proof they met, sire," said Richelieu. "But I think I can find proof, if your majesty will help me."

"Tell me! Anything!" cried the King.

"Give a fancy party, sire," the Cardinal said. "And tell the Queen to wear her diamond necklace—the one you gave her."

"It will be done, Richelieu," said the King.

As soon as Richelieu left, Louis XIII sent for the Queen. He did just as Richelieu had said. When he told the Queen that she *had* to wear the necklace, he couldn't miss the look on her face. She seemed scared to death. When she was gone, the King thought to himself, "Richelieu was right. I never saw her so scared. But what is this all about?"

Back in her room, the Queen threw herself onto her bed and began to cry. She was still crying when Madame Bonacieux found her. A few minutes later, the Queen told Madame Bonacieux the whole story. "So, I must get the diamonds back," said the Queen, with tears in her eyes. "But they are in England. This could mean death for me. And war between France and England. Oh, Constance, what can I do?"

"You must write a letter to the Duke, madame," said Constance Bonacieux. "A messenger can go to England. Once the Duke reads the letter, he will give the diamonds back. And the same messenger can bring the stones back to you."

"But where can we find such a person?" asked the Queen. "He must be very brave. His life will be in danger. And we must be able to trust him . . . with our own lives."

"Don't worry, your majesty," said Constance Bonacieux. "I think I know such a man."

An hour later, she had told the story to young D'Artagnan. "Can you help me, and the Queen?" she asked.

"I would do anything," said D'Artagnan.

"Then take this sack," Constance Bonacieux said. "It contains gold—more than enough to get you to England and back. And God go with you!"

D'Artagnan kissed Constance Bonacieux's hand and rushed from the room. But what neither Constance nor D'Artagnan knew was that fat little M. Bonacieux was in the next room, listening. He smiled to himself and thought, "I must tell this to the Cardinal. He will pay me well for knowing this!"

7 Journey to London

A few days later, D'Artagnan and the three Musketeers set off for England. All four brought their lackeys, D'Artagnan's faithful Planchet, with Bazin, Mousqueton, and Grimaud, who worked for Aramis, Porthos, and Athos. All men carried swords and guns.

Traveling with three hot tempers is never dull, as D'Artagnan soon found out. They had just reached an inn in Chantilly, not far from Paris, when the troubles began. Porthos got into a fight with a stranger at the inn. In no time, swords were drawn.

"Go ahead without me," cried Porthos to the others. "It may take me some time to kill this fool. I'll join you later!"

The men rode on. Not long after they left the inn, Athos held up a hand. The riders stopped. Athos pointed to a group of men ahead. They were fixing the deep holes in the road.

"Look there," Athos said to D'Artagnan.

"I see it," D'Artagnan replied. "A road crew."

Athos took a small telescope from one of his saddlebags. "Look again," he told D'Artagnan. "See?

They are wearing work clothes, *over* uniforms of the Cardinal's men. It's a trap!"

"What will we do?" asked Aramis.

"It's the only road we can take," Athos said. "We'll have to ride through them. If we gallop, some of us may get by."

Athos was right. As soon as the "road crew" saw the horsemen, they dropped their shovels. They ran to some bushes and took out guns. The Musketeers galloped by as hot lead whistled around them.

Aramis was hit in the shoulder. Mousqueton was grazed and knocked off his horse. And no one could stop for him. But the rest of them got through. Aramis was hurt pretty badly, so they dropped him off at the next inn they came to. Bazin, Aramis's lackey, stayed with him. Then Athos, D'Artagnan, and their lackeys galloped on.

Late that night, the four remaining men came to the town of Amiens. There was an inn in the town. Planchet took care of the horses. And because there was so much danger, Grimaud, Athos's lackey, slept outside their door. Athos and D'Artagnan had just gotten to bed when they heard noises from downstairs.

They came down to find Grimaud with his head all bloody. Someone had sneaked up on him. "That does it," said D'Artagnan. "Somebody knows what

we're doing. It can't be an accident that we've found trouble every step of the way."

"I think you're right," Athos said. "Let's pay the bill and get out of here. It's too dangerous to stop anywhere."

D'Artagnan gave the man who ran the inn some of the money from the sack Madame Bonacieux had given him. The innkeeper looked at the money. "It's fake money!" he cried.

"Don't be silly," said Athos. "The money is fine."

But the innkeeper kept shouting, "Fake money! Arrest them!"

All of a sudden, the door burst open. Four men with swords and guns came into the room. "Another trap!" cried Athos. "Run, D'Artagnan! I will stay and delay them!"

D'Artagnan ran to the stable. Planchet had two horses ready, and the two men got away. They rode the rest of the night to reach Calais. When they got there, they found a boat leaving for England. They got on the boat, and as it pulled away from Calais, D'Artagnan saw a group of armed men ride up to the waterfront. The Cardinal's men had come too late. Planchet and D'Artagnan had made it!

They had a little trouble getting around in London. Neither D'Artagnan nor Planchet could speak a word of English. But after a time, they found Buckingham's palace. As soon as the Duke

read the Queen's letter, he knew what was going on in Paris.

"Come with me," he told D'Artagnan. They went to the Duke's private rooms in the palace. He took out a heavy box with a lock on it. Inside was the jacket with the diamond buttons on it.

"Oh, no!" cried the Duke, looking the garment over. "Two of the diamonds are missing!" He frowned. "And I know who took them. And why!"

"But who, milord?" asked D'Artagnan.

"The Lady de Winter!" shouted Buckingham. "I wore them yesterday at a party for the King of England. Lady de Winter was all over me. She kept talking about what beautiful diamonds they were. Now, look here, D'Artagnan. See how the ribbons holding the buttons have been cut? She did that! And no doubt she is working for Richelieu!"

"But what are we going to do?" asked D'Artagnan. "The Queen must wear all twelve, five days from now. At the King of France's party. Where *are* the other two diamonds?"

"The Lady de Winter has them," the Duke replied. "But to catch the Queen, Richelieu needs the stones in France. She'll have to send them by the next boat to France."

"We are lost!" cried D'Artagnan. "We can't search every boat that leaves England."

"True," said the Duke with a smile. "But I am a very powerful man. I will do better than search every boat. I will *stop* every boat from leaving England! That way, at least you will get back to France before the stones do."

"But that still won't get back the two missing diamonds," D'Artagnan said.

"Nothing to worry about," said the Duke. "I am very rich. I'll buy two more diamonds just like the missing ones."

That is just what the Duke did. Two days later, D'Artagnan and the diamonds were in Paris.

8 The King's Ball

It was the fanciest ball of the year. The King of France had spent a fortune. Every important person in the country was there. As soon as the King arrived, Richelieu cornered him.

"Take this, your majesty," Richelieu said. He handed the King a small velvet box. There were two diamonds inside.

"Very pretty, Richelieu," said the King. "But what's going on? Why do you give me these two diamonds? And where did you get them?"

"Wait for the Queen to get here," said the Cardinal. "And see if she's wearing the diamond necklace that you gave her."

"She will be. I told her to," said the King.

"Very well, sire," said Richelieu. "Then, if she is, count how many diamonds are in her necklace. If there are only *ten*, I will tell you where I got these two."

Just then, Anne of Austria arrived at the ball. The King rushed up to her. She was wearing the diamonds. But there were twelve of them. Confused, the King gave the box to the Queen.

"Beautiful, Louis," the Queen said, smiling. "Now

I have *fourteen* perfect diamonds to wear. But where did you get them?"

"From the Cardinal Richelieu," said the King, now totally at sea.

"You must thank the Cardinal for me," said the Queen. Then she was off to dance with one of the guests.

The King went back to Richelieu. "The Queen thanks you for the diamonds," he told Richelieu. "And I'll thank you to tell me what's going on here!"

Richelieu knew he'd been beaten. He didn't know just how it had been done. But what could he say to the King? After thinking a moment, he put a big smile on his face and said, "I thought they'd be a nice surprise for the Queen, sire. They seemed to please her?"

"Yes," said the King. "But you had me give this big ball just so you could give her diamonds? She already has plenty of diamonds."

"So she does, sire," said Richelieu, hiding his feelings. "So she does. . . ."

A few hours after the ball was over, Constance Bonacieux took a message to D'Artagnan. "Follow me to the palace," she told the young Gascon. "Someone wishes to see you."

Once at the palace, she led D'Artagnan through a few secret stairways and into a dark room.

Suddenly, a hidden door opened. A long, beautiful arm of a woman reached inside. D'Artagnan knew who was at the other end of that arm: the Queen herself. He fell to his knees and kissed the hand. When the Queen took her hand back, D'Artagnan found she had given him a huge diamond ring. His money worries were over. He could live well for years on that diamond!

Once he got back from the ball, D'Artagnan looked for his friends. He hadn't seen any of them since he lost them on the way to England. It was hard to believe, but they were all right. Porthos had beaten the man in Chantilly. Aramis's shoulder wound was healing. And Athos had nothing more than a bad bump on his head. While he was fighting the four men in Amiens, someone had knocked him out. The Musketeers' three lackeys were all right, too. Even Mousqueton had made it back to Paris.

The four friends were having a good time when the news came. Someone had made off with Constance Bonacieux again. "But who . . . ? Why?" asked D'Artagnan.

"It wouldn't be Richelieu," Athos said. "He knows we beat him fairly. He won't forget, but he wouldn't try to get back at us through Madame Bonacieux." He thought for a moment, and then he went on, "It could be Richelieu's spy in England—the Lady

de Winter! From what you tell me about her, D'Artagnan, she is a bad enemy to have."

"I have never met Milady," said D'Artagnan. "I just know what the Duke of Buckingham told me. That she is fair haired, smart, beautiful, and as cruel as any man ever born."

"Wait a minute," said Athos. "I once knew a woman like that. . . . But no, it couldn't be. She is supposed to be dead."

Athos smiled and took a drink of wine. "No matter," he said. "Let's all have a good time tonight. And tomorrow, D'Artagnan, we will find your lovely Madame Bonacieux. . . ."

9 Milady

For the next few weeks, D'Artagnan tried to find his beloved Constance Bonacieux. He had no luck at all. It was as if the earth had swallowed her. Finally, he decided to see what he could find out from Lady de Winter, who was still in Paris.

D'Artagnan arranged to meet her and found that she was very charming. She was more beautiful than he had imagined. Milady acted as if she really liked D'Artagnan. And they started seeing each other almost every night. It wasn't long before young D'Artagnan was madly in love with her.

But Lady de Winter was still working for Rochefort. When she came to Paris with the two diamonds, she had hoped for great rewards from Richelieu. But in Rochefort's view, Milady had failed at her job, and he was angry. She secretly swore to get even with D'Artagnan and the three Musketeers.

D'Artagnan stayed hopelessly in love with Milady until he found out the truth from her maid. She told him that Milady really hated him and only pretended to be in love with him. Milady was leading him into a trap so that she could get even with him. D'Artagnan was angry, but he didn't let

Milady know that he knew the truth. He still wanted to find out what happened to Constance Bonacieux. But he never did.

D'Artagnan kept seeing Lady de Winter until a war broke out in the south of France. The city of La Rochelle, on the Atlantic coast of France, rose against the King. Most of the people in La Rochelle were Protestants. But the government was Catholic. In fact, that is why Richelieu had great power. As a Cardinal of the Catholic Church, he was also part of the French government.

The La Rochelle uprising gave England a chance to attack France, its enemy. England was a Protestant country. So the Duke of Buckingham sneaked arms and money to the Protestants in La Rochelle. The King and Richelieu couldn't have this. They sent a large army to take La Rochelle from the Protestants. And with that army were D'Artagnan and the three Musketeers.

After a few months, the battle at La Rochelle turned into a siege. There were walls around the city. The King's army couldn't get through. So they formed a camp, in the shape of a ring, all around the city. The people of La Rochelle couldn't get out. And their food and supplies couldn't get in. All the King's men had to do was wait until the Protestants at La Rochelle were hungry enough to give up.

But it took a long time. The Protestants had a lot of food and arms saved up for the siege. Richelieu went to visit the King's men to see how the fight was going. While D'Artagnan was in a different part of the camp, the three Musketeers got a strange job. They had to take Richelieu from place to place and see that he was safe. They didn't want to, but orders were orders.

The Cardinal went to a nearby inn, and went upstairs for a secret meeting with someone. The Musketeers stayed downstairs. "I wish I knew what was going on up there," said Athos.

"Why wish?" said Porthos, pointing to a chimney pipe that ran upstairs to a fireplace in the room above them.

"Why wish, indeed," said Athos, with a smile. He unhooked the chimney pipe. Suddenly, they could listen in on the talk upstairs. The Cardinal was talking to none other than Lady de Winter!

"You must go back to England," the Cardinal was saying to Milady.

"But I can't!" said Milady. "Buckingham won't forget I stole the two diamonds off his jacket. He'd put me in jail!"

"No, he wouldn't," said the Cardinal smoothly. "Because you are my personal messenger. And this is the message I'll send to him: If he goes on helping the Protestants in La Rochelle, I will tell everyone about his love affair with the Queen. Her name will be dragged through the mud. It might even cost her her life! That will make him listen."

"This is a very dangerous job," said Milady. "But I will do it, if you do one thing for me."

"Name it," said Richelieu.

"I want the life of young D'Artagnan," she said. "I thought I could get even by grabbing Constance Bonacieux. But I can't find her."

"And I know why," the Cardinal said. "The Queen thought you might harm Madame Bonacieux. So she's hidden her in a convent at Bethune."

"I should have known," said Milady. "But if I do this job, I want a *lettre de cachet.*"

A *lettre de cachet* was a very powerful piece of paper. With it, you could have anyone you wanted thrown in jail forever. There would be no trial. And what's more, no one outside would know. A *lettre de cachet* was a secret paper. This was how Milady would get even with D'Artagnan!

"If you can prove that D'Artagnan worked for Buckingham," said Richelieu, "the paper is yours."

"I'll give you more proof than you'll need," said Milady. "I will leave for London tonight!"

Athos got the chimney pipe back in place just as Richelieu came down the stairs. The three Musketeers didn't let on about what they had heard. They went back to the camp with the Cardinal. When they saw D'Artagnan, they told him what was going on.

"So, you've got to be very careful," Athos told D'Artagnan. "Milady is after your life."

"I don't care!" cried the young Gascon. "I must save Constance."

"Wait," said Athos. "There is more to the story. I haven't told you another thing."

"But we told him everything," said Aramis.

"Not all. When I heard Milady's voice, I knew who she was," said Athos. He smiled sadly. "How could I ever forget?"

"For God's sake, tell us," said Porthos.

"Let me tell you a story," said Athos. "Once, there was a young nobleman. He owned land and had many servants. He was very rich." The three others looked at each other and nodded. They knew Athos was talking about himself. But it hurt him too much to say it.

"One day, he met a beautiful lady," Athos went on. "He fell in love with her. He was told by his friends that the woman was no good. But he was in love and wouldn't listen. Until their wedding night. It was then that he saw the mark on her shoulder. From the Executioner of Lille . . ."

The three friends drew in their breaths. They knew what he meant. The Executioner of Lille was like the warden of a prison. Except when someone in the prison was put to death, he did it himself—with a huge two-handed sword. Those sentenced to death for awful crimes had a brand burned onto the skin of their shoulders. This was the mark Athos found on his ladylove. She was a criminal—maybe even a killer.

It was too late. Athos had married her. He had brought shame to his family name. So he turned the woman in. To make up for the harm he'd done to his family name, Athos joined the Musketeers and changed his own name.

"And all these years," Athos said, "I thought she was dead. But she is not."

"You mean Lady de Winter . . . ?" said D'Artagnan.

"Yes," said Athos sadly. "She is my wife. And she is more dangerous than a poison snake."

"I must go to Constance Bonacieux right away," said D'Artagnan.

"But you can't, my friend," said Athos. "As long as the siege of La Rochelle goes on, we must stay here and fight."

"Besides," said Aramis, "Milady is off to England to cause what trouble she can. The best we can do is hope the siege ends soon. Then we will go to the convent of Bethune together. All for one, and one for all!"

10 Justice Done

The siege of La Rochelle dragged on and on. One day, M. de Tréville arrived with some news. Milady was back in France! In England, Buckingham *did* have her arrested. But she had talked her jailer into letting her get away. After all, the jailer was a young man, and Milady was very beautiful. She even talked the man into stabbing Buckingham for her. The Duke was at death's door, even now, M. de Tréville told them. The Cardinal got what he wanted. No help would go to the Protestants at La Rochelle.

Athos told M. de Tréville what they had heard at the inn. Now that Milady was back in France, they feared she would try to kill Constance Bonacieux. After that, they were afraid she would come after D'Artagnan.

"Say no more," said M. de Tréville. "You don't have to stay in La Rochelle. Without Buckingham's help, the siege will soon be over. Get on your horses, and save Madame Bonacieux!"

The four friends didn't have to be told twice. They were off for the convent right away. They had no way of knowing that they were already too late. . . .

At the convent, a well-dressed woman came to the gates. She asked to see Madame Bonacieux. Because she had a letter from Cardinal Richelieu, they let her in. After all, Richelieu was a Cardinal. In a short time, Milady was alone with Constance Bonacieux.

"I have come to take you away," Milady told her. "D'Artagnan sent me to get you."

"I don't know . . . ," said Constance. She wasn't sure about this strange woman.

"You *must* believe me," said Milady. "If you don't come, you'll be in danger."

Constance still wasn't sure. But Milady turned on her charm. Finally, Constance said she would go with her. "Wonderful, my dear," said Milady. "Now, go get ready. I'll pour us some wine."

While Constance was getting her things together, Milady poured the wine. But into Constance's glass, she also poured a white powder from a trick ring she wore. When Constance came back into the room, Milady handed her the glass of wine. Constance drank it!

Just as she finished the last drop, they heard horses coming. "It's the Cardinal's men!" cried Milady. "We must hurry!"

"But I can't," said Constance. She could hardly stand up now. The poison was doing its work. "I feel so funny . . . ," she said. Then she fell to the floor. Milady laughed, and ran from the room.

Moments after Milady left, D'Artagnan and the Musketeers burst into the room. D'Artagnan rushed to Constance. Athos picked up the wine glass and smelled it. "Poison!" he said.

"Who did this?" cried D'Artagnan. "They will pay!"

At that moment, Constance opened her eyes. She saw D'Artagnan and smiled. Just before she died, she told D'Artagnan and the three Musketeers what had happened. She told them what the "nice strange lady" looked like.

"Milady!" growled Athos. "Let's go. Maybe we can still catch her!"

But D'Artagnan didn't want to leave Constance, even though she was dead. "Make sense, D'Artagnan," Athos told him. "You can't bring Constance back to life. But you *can* get her killer."

D'Artagnan didn't need to hear more. When he stood up from poor Constance's side, a change came over him. He was no longer the happy young Gascon, always ready to laugh. His face was a mask of hate. "Let's go," he said to Athos quietly.

The four friends found out from the nuns at the convent which way Milady had gone. She had

taken the road to Armentieres. By riding full out, they got to Armentieres a few minutes after Milady did. When they got off their horses at the inn, they faced a new danger. Milady was with ten soldiers of the Cardinal.

When he saw the Cardinal's men, D'Artagnan's heart raced. The leader of the Cardinal's men was Rochefort, the man with the scar!

"The game is over," D'Artagnan said to Rochefort. "We have a score to settle, you and I."

"I am ready," said the man with the scar, drawing his sword.

All over the yard of the inn, the two men fought. Athos had been right, D'Artagnan thought. Rochefort was one of the best swordsmen he'd ever seen. But D'Artagnan could not be stopped by anyone. His heart was filled with cold hate for Milady and her boss, Rochefort. He fought as he'd never fought in his life. The man with the scar fell, bleeding badly from a shoulder wound.

Then the four friends took on the other soldiers. True to form, after three were killed, the Cardinal's men ran. Then, Aramis, Porthos, and D'Artagnan went inside the inn and got Milady. She had a knife and tried to kill D'Artagnan. He took it from her, and they dragged her outside to where Athos waited.

On seeing Athos, Milady's eyes grew wide. "You!" she cried.

"Yes, my dear wife," said Athos. "But now we must take a long trip."

"Where are you taking me?" asked Milady.

"To see an old friend of yours," said Athos. "The Executioner of Lille."

"No, no!" screamed Milady. "He will kill me. . . . Please, wait. . . . Look here!" She pulled a piece of paper out of a pocket. Athos took it and smiled.

"Here you are," he said to D'Artagnan. "It is the *lettre de cachet*, signed by Richelieu himself. Keep this well, D'Artagnan. The Cardinal can never harm you again. Only the King is supposed to sign a *lettre de cachet*. You have caught Richelieu in the wrong. Now, let us be off for Lille."

"But you promised!" cried Milady.

"I promised nothing," growled Athos. "For what you did to me, I forgive you. God help me, I think I may still love you. But for what you did to Constance Bonacieux, you must pay."

They tied up Milady and carried her to Lille. Once the Executioner saw the mark on her shoulder, that was it. There was no trial. The mark meant she'd already had one. He took her into the prison, and in a few hours, had cut off her head. Athos couldn't watch. In a strange way, he still loved Milady.

But D'Artagnan watched to make sure Milady was dead. He could not forgive Milady for what she had done to his beloved Constance. Then,

together, the four friends rode sadly back to Paris. Porthos saw how upset both Athos and D'Artagnan were.

"Cheer up, my friends," he told them. "It's all over now. We have lost a few battles. We have won many. Now, we shall drink and try to forget."

But Richelieu didn't forget. A day after D'Artagnan was back in Paris, he got an order. The Cardinal wanted to see him. In a short time, he was shown into the Cardinal's office.

"Sit down, my boy," said Richelieu smoothly. "I wish to talk to you. I want to make you an offer."

D'Artagnan looked at Richelieu. The man had played a big part in the death of Constance. He'd told Milady where she could find her victim. D'Artagnan wanted to jump across the desk and kill him. But he could not. Richelieu was too important a man.

"What is this offer?" asked D'Artagnan.

"I want you to work for me," said Richelieu. "You have proved how brave you are. And how good you are with a sword."

"Never," said D'Artagnan. "In a short time, I will be a full Musketeer. I will serve France as my father did. As a Musketeer."

"Let me put it this way," Richelieu said, leaning forward. "You have killed many of my men. Rochefort lies wounded. Lady de Winter is dead. I have proof you worked for Buckingham. If you don't join me, I will have you put in prison."

"Oh, I don't think so," said D'Artagnan, with a smile. He took out the *lettre de cachet*. The Cardinal knew what it was right away. He smiled.

"Very well," he said to D'Artagnan. "I see what you have there. Nothing will happen to you. Go, join your Musketeers."

As D'Artagnan got up to leave, Richelieu said one more thing. "Young man," he said, "we have fought in the past. But that is over. You may not believe me, but I love France. I have done what I thought best. I know that you, too, love France. Go in peace, my boy."

The Cardinal kept his word. He never again was an enemy to D'Artagnan and the three Musketeers. They went back to La Rochelle, where they all fought bravely for France. In fact, after Rochefort recovered, a few times came when he fought at D'Artagnan's side.

When the siege ended, D'Artagnan became a full Musketeer. But his three friends decided to drop out of the service and go on to other things. Before they all went their separate ways, the four friends spent one last evening together.

"I'm tired of fighting all the time," said Aramis. "I will miss you all, but I have always wanted to be a priest. And now I shall do it."

"And what of you, Athos?" asked D'Artagnan.

"Now that Milady is dead," said Athos, "I can go back to my family and my land."

"And I," said Porthos with a laugh, "will do what I want."

"What's that?" they all asked.

"I am going to marry a very rich lady who will take care of me."

"So you won't have a patch in your pants?" asked D'Artagnan.

"Easy there," said Porthos, with a smile. "I never *did* fight you about that."

"But remember this, D'Artagnan," said Athos. "If you ever have any trouble, get word to us. We will come." He raised his wine glass. "To the *four* Musketeers," he said. "All for one, and one for all!"